The Flag

by Maryellen Gregoire

Nancy E. Harris, M.Ed—Reading
National Reading Consultant

capstone
classroom
Heinemann Raintree • Red Brick Learning
division of Capstone

I see a big flag.

I see a small flag.

I see a big flag.

NEW YORK STOCK EXCHANGE

I see a small flag.

I see a big flag.

I see a small flag.

I see a big flag.

Membership
For life.
SPORTS
AUTHORITY
UNDER ARMOUR

I see many flags!